THE
Joaquin Murrieta
LEGACY

by
LONNIE W. MOORE

Copyright © 1998
Lonnie W. Moore

All rights reserved. No part of this book may be
reproduced or transmitted in any form, or by any means,
electronic or mechanical, including photocopying,
recording, or by any information storage,
or retrieval system, without the permission,
in writing, from the Publisher.

ILLUSTRATIONS AND COVER:
Gregg Tillman and Craig Tillman

Ordering information in the back of the book.

ISBN 0-9661244-0-5

Printed in the USA by

MORRIS PUBLISHING
3212 East Highway 30 • Kearney, NE 68847 • 1-800-650-7888

DEDICATION

To Mom Moore, for always being there for me.

To my children, Rhonda Kerley, and Pamela Moore. My grandsons, Casey and Patrick Kerley, and Michael Moore, and grandaughter Loni Anne Moore.

To my sisters, Betty "Moore" Conti, Iola "Moore" Pair, and Lola "Moore" Croxdale "THE MOORE KIDS". Their children, grandchildren, and great-grandchildren.

Lastly, my sincerest thanks to my sister Iola "Moore" Pair, for without her love and inspiration this project would never have been completed.

And I looked, and behold a pale horse;
And his name that sat on him was death,
And hell followed with him.

                        Revelations Chaper 6-8

FOREWORD

In January, 1848, James Marshall was building a Mill for John Sutter, when he had the rare distinction of being the first man to pick up flakes of gold at Coloma. The news of gold being found did not bring the big rush until a year later. The rich foothill streams and mines, at that time, were strictly being mined by white miners and white settlers.

California, being a Mexican Province, naturally attracted numerous Mexicans to the gold fields. During 1848, and through to early 1849, the Mexicans outnumbered the whites two to one. This didn't help the already high racial tensions that were running rampant in the gold country.

In 1850 the California State Legislature passed a very controversial Law, called "The Foreign Miner's Tax Law". It was to make it nearly impossible for any Foreigner to mine gold in the California Region. For a Foreigner to mine for gold, in California, he or she must buy a license and have it renewed every thirty days. It was extremely difficult for anyone to pay $20.00 a month, at that time. The Mexicans resented the Tax the most, because less than three years ago they were the lawful Citizens of California. This Law would cause many Foreigners, mostly Mexicans, to leave the gold country. Many turned to robbing and killing just to try and escape the area.

It was during this time period, that we hear of a young Mexican, and some of his family, that were persecuted by the white miners and outlaws. This hard working, well mannered young man was about to become the most celebrated Mexican Bandido in California History, JOAQUIN MURRIETA.

CONTENTS

1. The Beginning 1
2. The Winds of Change...9
3. Oroville, Joaquin's Buried Treasure 17
4. Captain Harry Love, and California Rangers 23

    Poster announcing the exhibit of Joaquin's head......32
    Sworn Affidavit, of authenticity of head 33
    Summation 37
    Treasure map of Seven Falls, Oroville, California 39
    Reference material 40

THE BEGINNING

The year was 1850. The Mexican American War was over, but tensions were still high between the warring factors. California was a hotbed for Mexican and American outlaws and thieves. The gold rush had started and people from all over the world were pouring into California, in search of gold.

Most were God fearing men looking for the elusive promise land, some were outlaws preying on the hard working, law abiding citizens.

Gold was not unknown to Californians, prior to these times. There was gold discovered at Placerita Canyon, in early 1842, and many Sonorians came up to California during these days. Even though Sonorians were thought to be good miners, not all immigrants from that area were experienced miners. Most were young men, drifters, gamblers, and people just looking for what California had to offer.

In the Eastern part of the United States, the out cry, from published novels said, "Come, Come, young men. The rich valleys and mountains are virgin and virtually uninhabited." It was said that on the banks of the Feather River, you could scratch and dig big yellow chunks of gold right off the side of it's banks.

Many left crops in the fields. Homes unfinished, and family members standing on half finished doorsteps, waving goodbye.

Even though the many tragedys that had come before them, the thoughts of gold and riches erased everything in their minds. Not long before, the suffering of many settlers, trying to make their way west, were legend.

The first that comes to mind, were the Donner Party of 1846-1847. This had to be the most tragic of them all. Although these events were still fresh in their minds, the trek westward was all they yearned for. The ultimate dreams, from a Nation of dreamers, lay just beyond the next horizon.

Visions of fame and fortune were tugging at their hearts and minds. It was during these prosperous times that we first hear of a brash young man, from Sonora, Mexico. His name, JOAQUIN MURRIETA.

Joaquin Murrieta settled in Los Angeles, California in early 1850. He was eighteen years old, and the young man had the spirit of an Appoloosa stallion.

He was six feet tall. Gracefully built, and considered extremely handsome by the ladies he encountered. Joaquin hated the insecurity and the Revolutions that were every day occurances of Mexico. He decided to come to California, and seek his fame and fortune.

Joaquin Murrieta was a noted horseman. He fancied fine horse flesh. He, himself rode a beautiful light grey stallion. Sixteen hands high, with the gait of an Arabian, and the speed of a Thorobred.

For a man so young, in years, he was fast becoming the person to seek out for information on the best breeds of horses available, in the Los Angeles and surrounding areas.

Los Angeles, at this time, was a small Village with a Population of twelve hundred people. The area had become a Mecca for Mexican and American outlaws, due to the discovery of gold. The population of this part of California was mostly Spanish speaking. It was known for its gambling halls, whore houses, and had a rough and ready reputation.

Horse stealing and other forms of thievery were the main occupations of its settlers. Although the excitement of the Country was intriguing, Joaquin didn't feel comfortable.

Joaquin Murrieta was gaining the reputation of a dealer in fine horses when he met a beautiful young woman from New Mexico. Her name was Ana Beliz. Soon Ana became known as the woman of Joaquin. This was such a whirlwind romance, they soon decided to be married.

Ana was a beautiful young woman, twenty-two years old, and unknown to Joaquin had quite a reputation of her own. Joaquin did not know that Ana Beliz was, and had been, an informant, and whore, for the local Militia, for some time.

Joaquin was young, and had never been involved with an experienced woman. Being his first real love, he couldn't see past her lovely face. One afternoon Joaquin came home early, from the stables, and found Ana in bed with Juan Cardoza, a member of the local Militia. He was so stunned, he stood in the doorway, in disbelief at what he was seeing. Joaquin turned and walked away never to see Ana again. His heart was broken. His first real love had betrayed him.

He was deeply saddened by this turn of events, and after several skirmishes with the local Militia, he decided to head north to the gold fields to pursue his fortune. Little did he know what fate had in store for him.

Joaquin Murrieta had many friends in the Los Angeles area, that he had known from Sonora, Mexico. Among them were Reyes Feliz, and his beautiful sister Rosa. One rainy, and foggy evening Joaquin confronted them with a proposition. "Let's go north to the gold fields, and see how we can do." Reyes and Rosa thought that would be a great idea.

The Los Angeles area, was becoming such a Mecca for outlaws, and thieves, when a man was found murdered in the streets, immediatly the cry was, "KILLED BY MEXI-

CANS." They decided that any area, other than Los Angeles, would be fine.

Joaquin already had family and friends in several parts of the State, including San Andreas, San Juan, Marysville, and Mokelumne Hill.

Jesus Feliz, brother of Reyes and Rosa, joined with them. They all soon headed north towards Stanislaus Placers. After a couple of weeks of hard riding, they rode into Stockton, California.

Stockton was a town on the verge of great prosperity. Just a small ranch surrounded by tule marshes before 1848. Just before December 1849, one million dollars worth of building lots had been sold. Many nationalities were pouring into Stockton wanting to start a business. It was a time of great expansion and prosperity.

Thousands of immigrants and miners would flow into Stockton to outfit themselves for their journey into the gold fields of northern California. In 1848, when the Treaty of Guadalupe Hidalgo was signed, giving California to the United States, Stockton was one of the first small towns to prosper from the Treaty.

Joaquin Murrieta, the Feliz brothers, and Rosa, continued north to the Stanislaus Placers to pursue their fortune. After several days they rode into a very promising area of the Stanislaus. There was a stream running through this place, and an abundance of trees in which to build a cabin and corrals.

They set up camp and began going through the proper channels to get their claim working. Joaquin didn't want to do anything that would have the local authorities after them. Soon everything was going fine. Between them all there was plenty of work to do. It wasn't long before their hard work was starting to pay off.

Joaquin and Rosa had decided to get married, and settle down in this beautiful area they called home. They had known each other since childhood, and it seemed like best of friends would make best of lovers.

Within a few months they had built a small cabin and were starting to accumulate a small fortune in gold. Little did he realize that fate was about to deal him a terrible blow.

Joaquin and Rosa were very friendly and cordial, and were liked by everyone they encountered. With all the hard work and being such good neighbors, they had earned the respect and admiration of the whole community. They had made friends in the area and their new life together seemed destined for perfection.

The country, at this time, was full of cruel and desperate men. These men looked upon the Mexican population as conquered subjects of the United States. The outlaws and proverbial hell raisers, of the area, too lazy to work on their own, began to terrorize any Foreigner under the so called Foreign Miner's Tax Law. They thought that being a natural born Citizen, gave them the right to do so.

They had no authority or jurisdiction. They were just prejudice heathens, preying on simple miners and their families.

The Foreign Miner's Tax Law, although repealed in 1851, stated that every Foreigner would have to pay twenty dollars per month in order to mine for gold in California. This caused tremendous hardship on all who had to comply. The Mexicans were very resentful of the Law, and openly defied it.

The Foreign Miner's Tax Law proved that open prejudice was alive and well in California, even then. Even though most of the Mexican miners weren't successful in their mining ventures, it left behind a heritage of hatred and prejudice that would plague the people of California for generations to come.

It was late summer of 1850 when one such group of men paid Joaquin and Rosa a visit. The word was out that

Joaquin was working hard and fast putting together a small fortune in gold. His claim was very rich and although the work was very hard, it was paying dividends at a very fast pace.

When the men rode onto Joaquin's claim, he and Rosa were working on the corral. This defiant, drunken bunch told Joaquin he would have to give up his claim, because they didn't allow Mexicans to mine in their region. Joaquin, politely told them his Tax was paid, and he was not about to give it up.

This group of lawless men, having force in numbers to do so, began to beat Joaquin terribly. Rosa intervened and they began to assault her too. While on the ground, bleeding, and hurt badly, four of the assailants tied him up.

In full view of Joaquin, the other men proceeded to rape and beat Rosa, repeatedly. This inhumane act was devastating to Joaquin and Rosa. The men were laughing and drinking when they finally decided to leave. They yelled at Joaquin, as they were leaving, and told him to be gone, or when they returned they would kill him.

After several hours, Reyes Feliz, Rosa's brother returned from town to find them both beaten and near death. Reyes flew into a rage at what he saw. He began to help them into the cabin, and proceded to treat their wounds.

When Joaquin finally regained consciousness, they all had decisions to make. They decided for their own safety it would be best if they relocated to another area. Rosa loved their little cabin, but finally gave in to the pressures of Joaquin and Reyes. They knew the men would eventually come back, and kill them if they were still there. Rosa felt so dirty and ashamed, she could hardly face Joaquin.

The year of 1850, which was fast becoming a very eventful and profitable one for Joaquin and Rosa, ended with their family being ridiculed and disgraced by the outlaws and desperate men of the area. Their pursuit of family and fortune had been dealt a severe blow. The winds of change were blowing in a different direction.

This was one of many blows to Joaquin's pride. Once again, he was devastated by the acts of the outlaws.

He vowed to Rosa and himself, that nothing like this would ever happen again. Most of the people who knew Joaquin were outraged at his treatment. It was common knowledge through out the territory that these outlaws existed, and they were going around to immigrant camps and doing these kinds of ungodly sins, but everyone was afraid retaliation if they spoke up. If they made too much of a fuss, they could possibly be next. What the hell, it was just a bunch of Mexicans, anyway. This country was now owned by the United States of America and these sons a bitches were the Foreigners. Prejudice rang loud and clear in the minds of the new Californians.

The Joaquin Murrieta Legacy

THE WINDS OF CHANGE

In the year before the gold rush, never had there been an organized gang of Mexican Bandits in California. Many small groups of Mexican outlaws had done some damage around California, but most were caught or killed.

A new era was about to begin, that of THE LEGEND OF JOAQUIN MURRIETA.

Despite his young years, Joaquin Murrieta was a very likable and intelligent young man. Once the word spread throughout the area of his treatment, it didn't take long for his many friends and fellow countrymen to come to his rescue, and wanted to join forces with him. Joaquin was quick to reveal his anger toward all whites, and anyone who sided with them.

There were many Mexicans who were resentful of their treatment. They were looking for a leader. A DYNAMIC young leader was on the way.

It seemed that Joaquin was being robbed, swindelled, or beaten, at every turn. He had lost an estimated forty thousand dollars in gold due to the beating and robbery, at his venture in the Stanislaus Placers. Joaquin vowed his revenge on all miners, Chinese, French, German, but mostly Americans.

His demeanor had changed dramatically. His heart was full of rage and hatred. He made an oath to get revenge and his path would be marked with blood.

Joaquin Murrieta was about to keep his promise. 1850 would be the beginning of THE LEGACY OF JOAQUIN MURRIETA, CALIFORNIA'S MOST CELEBRATED BANDIDO.

Joaquin Murrieta attracted a hellish group of men, led by the notorious Manuel Garcia. Manuel was also known to the authorities as THREE FINGER JACK. Manuel Garcia was a cold blooded killer, without remorse, or feelings for his victims.

MANUEL, THREE FINGER JACK, GARCIA

Manuel Garcia was one of the most feared of all the gang members. He was a large man, very brave, and delighted in the art of killing. Manuel was also known as, Tres Dedos, in Spanish meaning three fingers. Many cruel and horrendous murders had been credited to Manuel Garcia. He was a true monster, and reveled in his reputation.

TEODORO VALENZUELA

Teohoro was the brother of Joaquin Valenzuela. He was an excelent horseman and drover. He could break the wildest horses, in the country. Not known as a killer, but very reliable when needed.

JOAQUIN VALENZUELA

Joaquin Valenzuela was much older than the others in the group. He was a known bandit, with a great amount of skill and experience.

He was also entrusted with very important duties by Joaquin Murrieta. For many years he was a bandit under the direction of Mexico's famous Guerilla Chief, Padre Jurata. He was later to become known as one of the five Joaquins.

JOSE OCHOA

Jose was given the duties of tending horses and was a dedicated lookout for other gang members. He was young and strong and a devoted gang member.

JUAN LOPEZ
Juan was a short, stocky, well-built man. Very crude but an excellent horseman. He had the nickname Juan Ears, because every man he killed he would cut off their left ear. He was a ruthless killer, and brazo debecho of Manuel Garcia.

PEDRO GONZALES
Pedro was a horse theif, extroadinaire. He kept the gangs supplied with a constant supply of fresh horses. Pedro was also a very young man, fearless, and a very skillful spy.

REYES FELIZ
Reyes was the brother of Jesus and Rosa. Devoted to Joaquin Murrieta.
He was very brave and impulsive. He hated the Americans for beating and degrading Joaquin and Rosa.

JESUS FELIZ
Brother to Reyes and Rosa, and also a great admirer of Joaquin Murrieta. The main job for Jesus was to take care of the ranch and to protect Rosa with his life. He also carried letters to family members and messages to other gang members.

CHAPPO
Chappo was a young Indian, raised with the Mexicans at the Mission at Monterey, California. He was an excellent horseman and tracker. He took care of the horses around the camp.

JOSE FRANCISCO CARAVANTES
Jose was noted as Joaquin Murrieta's top body guard. Excellent marksman with a gun, and deeply devoted to Joaquin.

LUPE CANTUA

Lupe was an excellent horseman and drover. He had a brother nearly identical in looks and size. Very versatile and talented. Extremely handy to have around.

DOMINGO CANTUA

Brother to Lupe. Fearless, and excellent horseman, and gun fighter. He could shoe and handle horses with the best.

JOAQUIN BOTELLAS

Listed as one of the five Joaquins. Excellent horseman and devoted to the cause. Very active in all the business involving gang activities.

CLAUDIO ACEVEDO

One of the gangs older members, Claudio was very sneaky and tenacious when it came to killing. One member noted, Claudio has the nobility of a rattlesnake.

JOAQUIN MANUEL CARRILLO

He was a half brother to Joaquin Murrieta. Very similiar in size and build. He was extremely devoted to Joaquin and the cause.

In September 1850, the terror began. In the early years of the gold rush, there were a few Mexican outlaw groups roving southern and central California, stealing horses and gold. None were organized or very successful. This scenerio was about to change.

Once the plans were made, Joaquin and his gang began terrorizing miners of every nationality in Amador, Calavaras, Mariposa, Sandreas, Butte and Yuba Counties. They were quite an articulate bunch to see. Joaquin, Rosa and Manuel Garcia leading the way, with all the members following close behind. They all wore hard brimmed hats, serapes, button sided trousers and heavy roweled spurs.

Winters were strong in northern California, so Joaquin and his men decided to go south. They knew of a place in the Coalinga area, called Cantua Creek. They had stolen three hundred horses and eighty thousand dollars in gold in two short months. The gang all headed south to Cantua Creek, to regroup. They desperately needed a place to store their horses and prepare them for the trip to Mexico.

Joaquin, Rosa and the Feliz brothers, headed toward the coast with Jose Caravantes riding shotgun. They would join the other gang members at Cantua Creek, in a few weeks.

Joaquin and Rosa bought a small ranch near the coast in a place called Niles Canyon, and made it their home base. It was a small ranch, but the location, and setting was beautiful. Rosa fell in love with the place and that was good enough for Joaquin.

They had been riding hard for the last few months, so Rosa decided to stay at the ranch, and her brother Jesus would stay and protect her. Joaquin, Reyes, and Jose headed south. They would go to Cantua Creek to help the other members ready the horses for their journey to Mexico.

Word had spread quickly throughout the gold country about a young Mexican named JOAQUIN MURRIETA, and his gang of cut throats, who were killing, stealing and ravishing everything and everyone in sight. The name Joaquin was quite common in California, in the 1850's. Anyone using that name was immediatly thought to be the accused outlaw and murderer.

Even though Joaquin Murrieta and his men had left Calavaras County, for the warmer weather of central California, posse's were still chasing them all over the gold country of northern California.

The Joaquin Murrieta Legacy

When Joaquin and his men rode into Cantua Creek, the view was unbelievable. There were horses spread all around the area, and the weather was beautiful. This was also Joaquin's first look at the amazing Las Tres Piedras, The Three Rocks. The Three Rocks are enormous, sandstone, and quartzite rising eighty feet in a shear wall on the west side of each rock.

On the top side of these completely bare slopes are several watering holes. The water in them is only fresh after rain storms. Severe wind, and rain storms, throughout the Centuries had carved small holes and caves in the rocks. This is mainly a habitat for birds and bats. From the top of these, weathered at an elevation of four thousand one hundred feet, one can look out over the entire valley. This was one of the main reasons this area was so impressive to Joaquin Murrieta. A lookout posted at the top of these rocks, could see dust from horses hooves, many, many, miles away in any direction.

Joaquin was so impressed with the surroundings, he called Manuel Garcia and Joaquin Valenzuela together for a meeting. More men were needed to maintain such a strong hold as this. Manuel Garcia and Joaquin Valenzuela, already known criminals, went off in search of men to help maintain and help with the task at hand. With their help and the Mexican underground, men began to pour into Cantua Creek in droves.

Excellent horses were plentiful in California, in the 1850's. Mexican and American families prided themselves in having the finest in pure bred stock. It was not a chore for the expert Mexican riders to steal eighty to one hundred horses in a single raid.

Joaquin Murrieta decided to drive horses back to his home area of Sonora, Mexico, and put together the largest horse ranch in all of Mexico.

This particular job was given to Teodoro Valenzuela. Teodoro was able to pick his own men, and being such an excellent horseman, would head them out to Mexico. Teodoro could drive up to three hundred horses at a time. They would eventually become the main stay of the horse business in Sonora, Mexico.

During the winter months, Joaquin put together five groups of men to rob claims and steal horses. Orders were given to all men to kill anyone that resisted or got in their way.

The decision was made for the five gangs to spread out over the most lucrative areas in the gold fields, and to rob and kill everyone that offered resistance.

1851 rolled in with a vengeance. The Miner's Tax Law was being repealed, but it was too late. The damage had already been done. Tensions were still running high between miners and Foreigners, and nothing was going to slow it down.

Joaquin Murrieta and his gangs ran rampant throughout the northern California gold fields, terrorizing Chinese, French, Germans, but mostly American miners. No one could stand in his way.

Some of Joaquin Murrieta's favorite hang outs were at Mokelumne Hill and Hornitos. Joaquin liked to play Monte at the Hornito's Saloon. Hornitos was a very tough little town, inhabited by outlaws and gun fighters. Monte was a game of chance that attracted men of that era, like magnets. Joaquin played the game very well. He loved to play Monte. It was his way of taking his mind off the business at hand. Joaquin had a lot of friends in Hornitos, but after a few days of rest and relaxation, he was back on the trail.

The authorities could not figure out how Joaquin could be in so many places at the same time. The gangs were spread out between San Andreas, Murphy's Camp, Jackson, Marysville, and they just went from area to area robbing miners and stealing horses. There was a steady stream of stolen horses between northern California and Cantua Creek. Once there, they were branded with the Tres Piedras Brand. Then they were delivered to Sonora, Mexico.

OROVILLE

JOAQUIN MURRIETA HID SOME BURIED TREASURE

Things were going very well for Joaquin and his men. It was very lucrative and satisfying for them all. Although things were going well, it was not always so easy.

Some of Joaquin's escapes, under a barrage of gunfire, were considered miracles. It was as though he were living a charmed life.

In November of 1851, Joaquin and his gang of Mexican Terrorists, robbed, killed, and mutilated several people, including the Sheriff of Yuba County. They were north of Marysville, at the time, heading toward Oroville, and the Feather River.

Joaquin loved the beauty of the Feather River, and during this operation he hid some gold in the area of the Feather River Canyon.

Joaquin Murrieta had a great love for the outdoors. The many Lakes, Rivers, and streams around Oroville, brought extreme comfort to Joaquin. Many days and nights he would take time to enjoy a beautiful area of Northern California.

The Feather River was his favorite. It was a magnificent, unspoiled area of Northern California. The River, flowing unrestricted through the trees and rocks, made an unforgetable and soothing sound.

The small group made their camp in an isolated area. Joaquin knew his supplys were running low, so he chose a trusted follower to go into the town of oroville and get what they needed when they traveled high up into the Feather River Canyon.

When the rider returned he told Joaquin and the group stories he had heard in Oroville, and how the town was bustling with miners outfitting for another quest to find gold along the Feather River. He had stopped in the Ophir Saloon, and heard talk about a disasterous flood that flooded Oroville the winter before. Half the town had been burned to the ground, and rebuilt. He found all their supplies at the Pioneer Grocery. He also told Joaquin that he heard that Oroville was the wickedest town in California, since it had more saloons than any other town in the State.

In the Saloon, men were talking about the killing and mutilation of the Yuba County Sheriff. Word traveled fast even in those days. They talked about the Joaquin Murrieta gang on the run.

Early the next morning, Joaquin and his men traveled deep into the Feather River Canyon. They knew a Posse was searching for them, so this was the perfect place to hide out for a while. As they traveled deeper, and higher, into the Canyon they were in awe of the beauty they saw. They found a hidden beauty before their eyes, a cascading water fall. It was called The Seven Falls of the South Branch, that was hidden from most. The waterfalls dropped in a series of seven falls plunging for a distance of over 500 feet, located deep in the Canyon of the Middle Fork of the Feather River.

Because the terrain was so steep, the Canyon walls hid the Falls. There was evidence prospectors had once been there searching for gold.

Joaquin had amassed forty seven thousand dollars in gold dust, from their thievery in Marysville. He knew the weight of the gold dust would slow them down if they had to travel fast.

In searching the area, near the falls, Joaquin found a small cave. He felt this was the ideal place to hide his gold. It was such a dense area, he knew it would be safe here, until he could return.

It was at this time, he ordered the gang to pack up, saying they would separate and rendezvous back at the Arroyo Cantua. Winter was close, and the winter of 1851 was one to remember. The snows in the Sierras was much deeper than usual. Every stream became a river. It was a tremendously hard winter in Northern California for everyone involved.

During the restful times his mind would wander back to Ana Beliz, and how it might have been in Los Angeles. He loved Rosa deeply, and knew there would never be another woman in his life.

Joaquin and Rosa were making a beautiful horse ranch out of their property at Niles Canyon. Everyone in the area thought this was a very nice young couple building themselves a future in the horse trading business.

They were invited to the most exquisite, gala events in the area. They always accepted as Senor and Senorita Joaquin Carrillo. Even in their Socializing, with the rich and prosperous, the main topic of conversation was how the violence and corruption was becoming so common in California.

A strange breed of men were still coming into California, thousands at a time. Hunger was causing even decent men to become thieves. The stories of gold nuggets as big as your fist were becoming few and far between. Even the ones who were doing quite well, their expenses were staggering.

Every necessity had to be packed into the hills from the cities far below. Eggs were one dollar each, and flour one hundred dollars a barrel. What little gold the men found was spent faster than they could accumulate it. Mining was no simple affair. It was very hard work, and you had to watch your back side at all times.

The gold fields were known as "The oneryest place this side of hell." Sonora, California boasted as having more whores, drunks, gamblers, and the largest chunks of gold in California. To say it was a thriving community, would be very conservative.

Joaquin had left Rosa with her brother Jesus at the Niles Canyon Ranch. He headed South to the Arroyo Cantua to reorganize his men. Upon arriving he was, once again, amazed at how well things were going. In such a short time they had amassed a fortune in gold, and the finest horses in the land.

1852 started as the year before. Joaquin was still waking up in the middle of the night screaming at the vision of his lovely Rosa being raped and beaten by the drunken cowards at Stanislaus Placers. This only seemed to intensify his hatred towards the Americans.

His reign of terror was getting bloodier and more intense as the days went by. Joaquin was considered a Mexican Revolutionist by the California Legislature, and needed to be stopped.

Joaquin Murrieta and his gang had already killed more people than any other outlaws in California History. Although his Legend was wide spread and growing everyday, Joaquin still yearned for Rosa and the style of living he enjoyed at the Niles Canyon Ranch.

Things were going so well. He and Rosa were adjusting to a life-style only dreamed by most. Joaquin was very loyal to his men and had promised them the same luxuries that he was enjoying.

The next few months were very busy and profitable, for Joaquin Murrieta and his gangs. Revenge was no longer the only thing on Joaquin's mind. His desire with getting the rest of his men financially secure was becoming his obsession.

The French, Chinese, and American miners suffered tremendously. The desire for revenge was no longer a factor. Gold and horses were the main concern.

The American River, Mokelumne Hill, and the Placerville area, seemed to have the most activity during this time. Joaquin and his men continued their onslaught on miners in these areas.

Joaquin seemed blessed with a sixth sense, and knew his time was possibly running short. No one could continue this type of activity without making some mistakes. He could feel the pressure starting to build.

The Joaquin Murrieta Legacy

CAPTAIN HARRY LOVE AND HIS CALIFORNIA RANGERS

The California Legislature didn't have a clue to who these gangs of men were. They knew the name of "JOAQUIN" and had heard all the horror stories, but really had no idea what to do. The Authorities were baffled also. The name Joaquin and all who were called by that name were all in extreme danger. Anyone with that name was immediately under suspicion, or would be killed instantly by the Authorities.

Joaquin Murrieta, had never been captured, or convicted of any crime, yet he was the most wanted Mexican in the land.

Mining was such hard work, and the riches were few and far between. A very small percentage of the people who came to California, for the gold rush, were sucessful. Also to the miners chagrin, there were many tales that were false. One particular one was "THE GREAT GOLD LAKE HOAX".

An old miner at Murphy's Diggings, told a story of a beautiful Lake that had been discovered near the Middle Fork of the Feather River. He told of huge gold nuggets that lay on the beach and shores. The sun would hit the shore, in early morning, and damn near blind you. Thousands of miners heard the story. The word spread like wildfire throughout the Region.

Although the Feather River was quite rich with gold, in the 1850's, this particular hoax was just a figment of an old miner's imagination. Many stories circulated throughout the gold fields, in the 1850's, some were true, but most of them were false.

In January 1853, Joaquin and his men left Calavaras County and headed towards the mining camps of San Andres. San Andreas, at this time, was one of the richest areas of the Mother Lode. Joaquin and his men ran rampant over the Chinese and other miners of the area. Joaquin was taking his vengeance out on anyone and anything in his path.

By this time, Californians were really becoming concerned. Newspapers, throughout the State, were begging the Authorities to protect the Citizens of California. The cry was, "SOMETHING HAS TO BE DONE WITH THIS OUTLAW JOAQUIN".

The more influential people, and the Press, kept telling Officials, "We need action taken immediatly." Finally, in the Spring of 1853, the Legislature made it's move. Their first Proposal was, that the State would offer "Five Thousand Dollars" reward for Joaquin Murrieta, dead or alive.

Mr. Covarrubias, of the Committee on Military Affairs, was outraged. His feeling were, that to set such a reward for a man who had never been convicted of a crime, was ridiculous. Also, such a reward would cause men to bring any Mexican before the State, just to try and get the reward.

Since no one really knew what Joaquin really looked like, it could be too easy. The California Legislature, finally listened, and instead of the reward, they passed an Act authorizing a dynamic man from Texas, HARRY LOVE, to raise a company of Rangers. This Act became Law on May 11, 1853.

Captain Harry Love and his Rangers, immediately went in search of the Heathen, Joaquin Murrieta. Governor Bigler gave Captain Love ninty days to find and kill Joaquin Murrieta.

Harry Love was a Veteran of Indian Warfare, and was involved with many Border conflicts along the Rio Grande. During the Mexican War, he was an important Soldier under the command of General Zachary Taylor. After the War, like so many others, Harry Love could hear the call of the California Gold Fields. He eventually settled in Mariposa County and was a part-time miner and Professional Bounty Hunter.

When Governor John Bigler, the California Legislature, and the Committee on Military Affairs, appointed Harry Love, everyone was really impressed. His courage and flawless record were without dispute.

Harry Love was a huge man. Six feet five inches tall, weighing two hundred pounds. A Reporter once wrote, "Harry Love is half man, and half Grizzley Bear."

Hiding behind the Authority given to him by Governor John Bigler, and the California Legislature, Captain Love began his pursuit of Joaquin Murrieta.

Harry Love was actually a hired killer for the State of California. One of Captain Love's favorite sayings was, "The only good Mexican, is a dead Mexican." Even though Harry Love was a Scout, and one time member of the Texas Rangers, he was quickly gaining his reputation for his fearless pursuit of Joaquin Murrieta. He constantly referred to Joaquin as, "That Mexican son of a Bitch."

Captain Harry Love and his Rangers, searched frantically, in every known area that Joaquin and his gangs had frequented. Captain Love and the California Rangers, were themselves, terrorizing Mariposa County, at this time. They were capturing Mexicans, taking their horses, gold, and cattle, and any other possessions of value. If they put up a fight or balked, in any way, they would be hung or shot on sight.

It was too much trouble to carry prisoners around with them, so when they were thought to be bandits, or revolutionist, they were usually just shot and left for the buzzards. They could always blame it on someone else.

Captain Harry Love's determination to capture Joaquin Murrieta was becoming an obsession. Ninty days wasn't enough time with which to capture Joaquin, and he did have a reputation to uphold.

The pursuit of Joaquin Murrieta and his gangs was becoming more and more frantic, as the days went by. Captain Love and his men rode day and night to find the illusive Joaquin.

TO AUTHORIZE THE RAISING OF A COMPANY OF RANGERS THE PEOPLE OF THE STATE OF CALIFORNIA, REPRESENTED IN SENATE AND ASSEMBLY, DO ENACT AS FOLLOWS:

SECTION 1.

Captain Harry Love is hereby authorized, and empowered, to raise a Company of Mounted Rangers, not to exceed twenty men, and Muster them into the Service of the United States for a period of three months, unless sooner disbanded by order of the Governor, for the purpose of capturing the party or gang of robbers, commanded by the five Joaquins, whose names are Joaquin Muriati, Joaquin Ocomorenia, Joaquin Valenzuela, Joaquin Botelleir, and Joaquin Carillo, and their banded associates.

SECTION 2.

Said Rangers shall furnish, at their own expense, the necessary horses, arms, equipments, ammunitions, provisions, forage, and for the purpose named in the first Section, and shall receive from the State of California the sum of one hundred and fifty dollars, each, per month, while in actual service during said three months, which shall be in full payment for all services rendered under the provisions of this Act.

SECTION 3.

The Comptroller of the State is hereby directed to Audit the accounts of said Rangers for their services, upon certificate of their Commander, and shall draw his Warrent upon the Treasurer of State, who is directed to pay the same out of any monies in the Treasury, not otherwise appropriated.

SECTION 4.

It shall be the duty of the said Rangers upon taking any prisoners, to deliver them safely to the County Authorities for trial, and upon making recovery of any stolen cattle, horses, or other property, to deliver the same to the Authorities of the county within which they may have been taken, and public notice shall be given as required by Law.

APPROVED, May 17, 1853

PERSONNEL LIST 1853 CALIFORNIA RANGERS APPOINTED BY GOVERNOR BIGLER:

Harry Love	Agustus Black
W.J. Henderson	C. Bludworth
T.J. Howard	John White
W.J. Howard	Bill Burns
Ed Campbell	Ed Connor
Dr. Hollister	George Chase
George Nuttall	Ned Van Burn
Jim Norton	Nick Ashmore
Bob McMasters	John Sylvester

They were baffled at the thought Joaquin could be at Murphy's Diggings one morning, and the Feather River area that same afternoon.

It was looking as though the ninety day enlistment would be over before Captain Love and his California Rangers would even find Joaquin, much less be lucky enough to kill him.

With the newly formed California Legislature under fire from the Citizens, Captain Love and his Rangers continued their onslaught. Now the Mexican population was under attack from a new force of outlaws, disguised as Lawmen.

The California Rangers were tenacious in their pursuit to find Joaquin Murrieta. The word had spread to all parts of California that Captain Harry Love and the California Rangers were hunting Joaquin. Just the sight of Harry Love struck fear into the hearts of every Mexican in the State.

They knew of his obsession to get Joaquin Murrieta. They also knew they had no idea of what he really looked like. Their only real clue was the pale grey stallion, that he rode. There was a classic confrontation on the horizon. Cries of "Remember the Alamo" from Harry Love and "Viva Mexico" coming from Joaquin and his men.

Joaquin and his men decided to let things cool down a little in the Northern part of the State. They knew Harry Love was pursuing them with a vengeance. They rode South to the Arroyo Cantua area. There was plenty of work to be done there. Horses had to be branded, and made ready for the trip to Mexico.

The gang members at Arroyo Cantua, were relaxed and felt very secure in their hideaway. It was a great time for drinking and telling stories of their conquests.

Harry Love finally got the break he was looking for with the capture of Jesus Feliz. Jesus traded his knowledge of the whereabouts of Joaquin Murrieta for Amnesty.

The Joaquin Murrieta Legacy

The next night, the California Rangers rode fifty miles into the heart of the Coast Range. It was here they would rest while they sent out small parties to scout the surrounding area. A few days later Captain Love and his men rode upon a camp of some seventy-five or eighty Mexicans. In their possession was about eight hundred horses. These were not Mustangs, they were some of the finest breed of horses to be found anywhere.

The Mexicans made no resistance, so Captain Love told them he was looking for Joaquin Murrieta. Being outnumbered, he decided to retrace his route and hold up in a near by station. The next day he returned with his full force of men, but the area was completely deserted. Discusted with his miscalulations, they decided to trail the herd of horses, South.

It was dusk when one of the Rangers spotted smoke from a campfire, in the distant plains. The Rangers immediately rode toward the smoke. They got within two hundred yards of the camp before they were spotted.

Immediately some of the Mexicans started running towards their horses and grabbing their rifles. One of the Rangers recognized a man he thought was Joaquin Murrieta. "There he is. There he is." yelled the Ranger. Realizing that they were recognized, as the Murrieta Gang, they began firing at the Rangers.

For the next thirty minutes, the fire of Hell descended upon Arroyo Cantua. Men were running in every direction. The sound of gunfire was exploding everywhere. Manuel Garcia retreated, on foot, and was fighting desperately when he was hit by several shots from the shotguns of the Rangers. Two other Mexicans fell beside him in a hail of gunfire. It was percieved, a miracle that Joaquin Murrieta had escaped through the brush, and made it on foot to the Las Tres Piedras, and held up there until the fighting had-ceased.

The weather was horrendous, at the Arroyo Cantua, that day. One hundred and fifteen degrees and a slight dusty wind was blowing from the west. This area of California is known for it's extreme heat, but today was hotter than ever before.

Captain Harry Love and his Men, were rounding up Prisoners and horses, when they decided that if they took the head of Joaquin Murrieta, and the hand of Manuel, "Three Fingered Jack", Garcia, that would be plenty of proof for Governor Bigler to issue their rewards.

The procedure began by taking off the hand of Manuel Garcia. They put it into a bottle of Spirits to preserve it. The next procedure was a little more difficult. Which one of the Son-of-a-bitches is Joaquin Murrieta? Amazingly, no one seemed to know. Lying just to the left, in a clump of brush was the young Indian Chappo. Immediately, Captain Love said, "Here's that Mexican Son-of-a-bitch." One of the Rangers jumped from his horse and began the horrorifying deed. Chappo's head was then put in a jar of Spirits, and the celebration began.

Joaquin was devastated by the sight of his men at the Arroyo Cantua. The word spread quickly of the massacre at Arroyo Cantua. The members of the Joaquin Murrieta Gang, that did survive, were running for their lives. The members that didn't seek refuge, in the Los Angeles area, quickly made it for the Border, and on to safe ground in the Province of Sonora, Mexico.

The majority of the members of Joaquin Murrieta's Gangs were dead. Captain Love and the California Rangers headed North to make their situation known to Governor Bigler and the California Legislature. Their prize was encased in two jars of Spirits. The supposed head of Joaquin Murrieta, and the hand of Manuel, "Three Fingered Jack" Garcia.

The Joaquin Murrieta Legacy

Even though no one really knew what Joaquin Murrieta looked like, they did recognize the hand of Manuel Garcia.

The jars were put on display in Stockton, California on August, 1853. Captain Love and his men had collected their reward, and had told some, not so true tales, to the California Legislature, and Governor Bigler.

It's true, that Manuel Garcia had been killed, and the hand in the jar was his, but the head in the other jar was that of "CHAPPO", a young Indian horseman, and devoted follower of Joaquin. It was not JOAQUIN MURRIETA.

Although the crys of foul were heard through-out the State, the reward was still paid. The jars, with the head and hand were very popular displays for years to come.

Captain Love had quite a few people sign Affidavits to the Authenticity of the head of Joaquin Murrieta. These people were all unreliable and Captain Love had swindeled the State of California.

Captain Harry Love and his Rangers had worked very hard. Their pursuit of the outlaw, Joaquin, was tenacious. He had earned the respect and admiration of all the Citizens of California.

Many Newspapers and noted people, of the State of California, were calling this a farce. One of the most notable was the San Francisco, ALTA.

On August 23, 1853, the San Francisco ALTA Newspaper recorded the following:

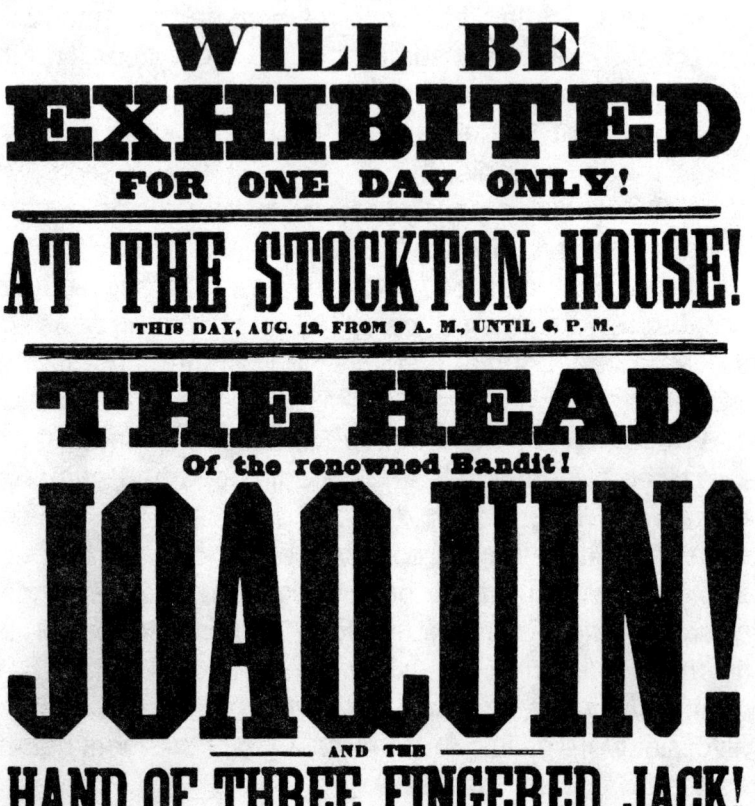

"JOAQUIN" and "THREE FINGERED JACK" were captured by the State Rangers, under the command of Captain Harry Love, at the Arroyo Cantua, July 24th. No reasonable doubt can be entertained in regard to the identification of the head now on exhibition, as being that of the notorious robber, Joaquin Murrieta, as it has been recognized by hundreds of persons who have formerly seen him.

It affords amusement to our Citizens to read the various accounts of the capture and decapitation of the Notorious JOAQUIN MURRIETA. The Humbug is so transparent, that it is so surprising that a sensible person can be impressed upon. A few weeks ago, a party of Native Californians, and Sonorians, started for the Tulare Valley for the express purpose of running Mustangs. Three of the party have returned, and reported that they were attacked by a party of Americans, and that the balance of the party, four in number, had been killed, and that Joaquin Valenzuela, one of them, was killed endeavoring to escape, and that his head was cut off, and held as a trophy by his captors. It is too well known that Joaquin Murrieta was not the person killed by Captain Harry Love's party at Panoche Pass. The head exhibited in Stockton bears no resemblance to that individual, and this is positively asserted by those who have seen the real Murrieta and the Spurious head. All accounts wind up by recommending the continuance of Love's Company in Service all right. The term of Service was about to expire, and although I will not say that interested parties have gotten up this Joaquin Expedition, yet, such expeditions can generally be traced to have an origin with few Speculators. Every murder and robbery, in the Country, has been attributed to "JOAQUIN". Sometimes it is Joaquin Carrillo that has committed the crimes, sometimes, Joaquin something else, always JOAQUIN.

SIGNED AND SWORN AFFIDAVITS TO THE AUTHENTICITY IF THE HEAD CLAIMED TO BE THAT OF JOAQUIN MURRIETA:

1. SUSAN BANTA, Mariposa County   August 8,1853
2. JOSE VAGA, Mariposa County   August 7,1853
3. PEDRO MONTEA, Mariposa County   August 7,1853

4. HENRY LONG, Mariposa County   August 7, 1853
5. JOHN GREEN, Mariposa County   August 7, 1853
6. WILLIAM BYRNES, Mariposa County   August 8, 1853
7. STEPHEN BOND, Mariposa county   August 8, 1853
8. JULIET THORP, Mariposa County   August 8, 1853
9. REV. DOMINIC BAINE, San Joaquin County August 11, 1853
10. HENRY MC CARGAR, San Joaquin County   August 11, 1853
11. DR. N.B. HUBBELL, San Joaquin County August 12, 1853

Even though the crys of FOUL were heard far and wide, the California Legislature stood behind the results. Many people had come forward, after the Battle Of Cantua, to say they had seen Joaquin Murrieta, and he was still in possession of his head.

Joaquin Murrieta had made another miraculous escape. It was as though God had let him have another chance at living the life he had originally pursued.

Joaquin had found one of the horses, and made his way back to the Niles Canyon Ranch, and the safety of his other way of life. Before he left Cantua, he buried his friends who were left for the buzzards by Harry Love, and the California Rangers.

Rosa had heard of the Battle, and the news of Joaquin's death. When she saw him riding in, she knew God had spared him for her. Now, that it was over, they had to make plans for a new beginning.

Joaquin and Rosa sold everything they had. The Ranch, horses, and a number of prized possessions. Within two weeks they had boarded a Cruise Ship, out of San Francisco for Mexico City, under the name of Carrillo. Joaquin Murrieta had made another miraculous escape.

Revenge was sweet and also very profitable for Joaquin and Rosa. They continued to live a very luxurious life for the next thirty years, as a reputable Ranch owner in Mexico City. He was known for breeding the finest horses in Mexico.

Joaquin knew he would never be able to return to Oroville and go deep into the feather River Canyon to retrieve his Gold Dust he had burried in a cave, near Seven Falls. As the years past, and he lived the life of contentment, he forgot all about the Oroville Gold.

During this time Captain Harry Love and his California Rangers were the toast of California. Everywhere they went they were treated like Royalty. The finest food, drinks, and most beautiful ladies, in California, were at their beck and call.

Although many disputed the fact that the particular head in a jar of Spirits was that of Joaquin Murrieta, praise was being poured out on Captain Harry Love. He was becoming a Legend on his own. He was being showered with gifts and praise from every corner of the State. He was a hero in the hearts and minds. The thing that haunted him most was, deep inside he knew he didn't get Joaquin Murrieta.

Captain Harry Love went to his grave with this eating at his very soul. The Lord moves in mysterious ways, and the last celebration belonged to JOAQUIN MURRIETA.

THE END

The Joaquin Murrieta Legacy

SUMMATION

Is there some Gold of Joaquin Murrieta's still hidden in California? I think there is. There has never been any documented proof of anyone stumbling upon a Cache of Gold Dust in California. Deep in the Feather River Canyon, above Oroville, at a place called Seven Falls, would be a great place to spend some time searching. Joaquin Murrieta camped up near the Seven Falls, while being chased by a Posse from Yuba County.

Another great place to search would be, Las Tres Piedras area North of Coalinga. This is a well documented area of Joaquin Murrieta's adventures. This area is twenty-five miles Northwest of Kettlemen City. I think this is another great place to spend some time with the Gold Detector.

The life of Joaquin Murrieta was a storied one, to say the least. Just the idea of a young Mexican, coming to California, in 1850, and by the end of 1853 was considered a Legend. I know he went from a nice, well-mannered, young man, into an extreme outlaw, and killing machine, but do we dare think of what may have happened if everything had gone the way he had planned? With his dynamic personality, and intelligence, could he have become Govenor of California, or President of these United States?

His assets were growing quickly, and with a little luck would have been a very rich young man. He was well educated, and was a very Prominent Citizen.

How many others have crossed the border, into California legally, or illegally, and were never given a chance?

The BAKERSFIELD CALIFORNIAN Newspaper, on Labor Day weekend, 1997 quoted, "The number of Illegal

Mexicans coming across the Border has dropped this year to 105,000."

In response to that quote, In the same Newspaper, same day, a quote from Jesus Silva-Herzog, Mexican Ambassador to the United States, said, and I quote, "We are recovering our lost Territories. We are doing it slowly, of course, but with a tremendous advantage, ALL THE LAND IS NOW PAVED."

GOD BLESS AMERICA

TREASURE MAP

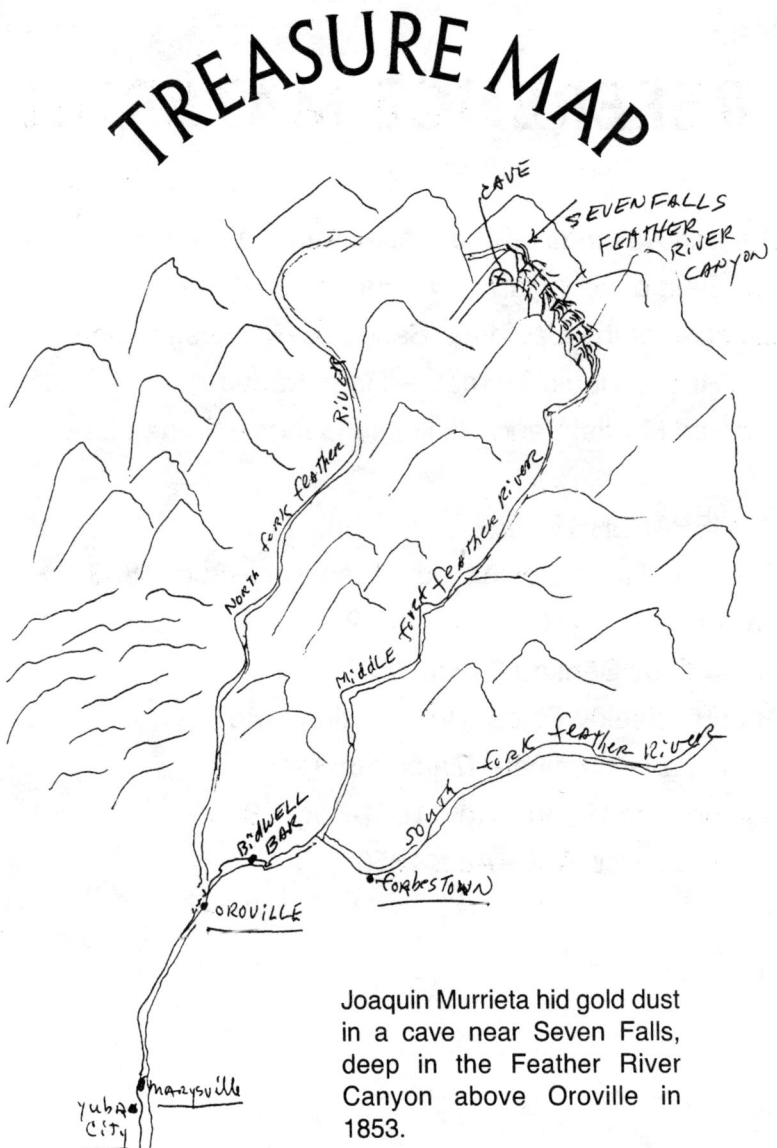

Joaquin Murrieta hid gold dust in a cave near Seven Falls, deep in the Feather River Canyon above Oroville in 1853.

REFERENCE MATERIAL

Life and Adventures of Joaquin Murrieta—John Ridge
The Best of Bret Harte—W. Harper, A. Peters
Legends of the California Bandidos—Angus Maclean
The Real Joaquin Murrieta—Remi Nadeau
Joaquin Murrieta and his Horse Gangs—Frank Latta

NEWSPAPERS

Stockton-San Joaquin Republican—Jan-Aug. 1853
California Police Gazette—1859
Santa Cruz Sentinel—Oct. 1856
Auburn Weekly Placer Herald—July, 1851
Calavaras Chronical—March 1853
Sacramento Union—Nov. 1851-Aug. 1853
San Francisco Alta—Aug. 1853

THE MURRIETA LEGACY

With the discovery of gold in a California stream, in 1848, America was instantly ushered into the chaotic Era of the gold rush. Word spread like wildfire throughout the world. A strange and mixed breed of men and women came to California, in the search of their fortune. Even though the raw beauty of California was such a treat, to most newcomers, violence and corruption was becoming a daily lifestyle.

In just three short years, Joaquin Murrieta left a Legacy unparalleled in the History of California. Gold, in the 1850's sold for sixteen dollars an ounce. At today's prices, there is a fortune in gold hidden in several places around the State. From the beautiful FEATHER RIVER area of OROVILLE, to hot, rolling, foothills of COALINGA.

JOAQUIN MURRIETTA'S FORTUNE
WAS NEVER FOUND

ORDER FORM

"THE JOAQUIN MURRIETA LEGACY"

by

LONNIE W. MOORE

Please send $12.95 check or money order
Price includes mailing costs

Send order to:

LONNIE W. MOORE
174 Oak Drive Parkway
Oroville, CA 95966
Phone: (530) 589-2881
Fax: (530) 589-3551

NAME _____

ADDRESS _____

_____

ORDER # OF BOOKS _____

AMOUNT ENCLOSED $ _____

Thank you